Jenny Mitchell

Map of a Plantation

Indigo Dreams Publishing

First Edition: Map of a Plantation
First published in Great Britain in 2021 by:
Indigo Dreams Publishing
24, Forest Houses
Cookworthy Moor
Halwill
Beaworthy
Devon
EX21 5UU

www.indigodreams.co.uk

Jenny Mitchell has asserted her right under the Copyright, Designs and Patents Act 1988 to be identified as the author of this work.
© Jenny Mitchell 2021

ISBN 978-1-912876-46-4

British Library Cataloguing in Publication Data. A CIP record for this book can be obtained from the British Library.

This book is sold subject to the condition that it shall not, by way of trade or otherwise, be lent, re-sold, hired out, or otherwise circulated without the author's and publisher's prior consent in any form of binding or cover other than that in which it is published and without a similar condition including this condition being imposed on the subsequent purchaser.

Designed and typeset in Palatino Linotype by Indigo Dreams. Cover design by Ronnie Goodyer. Cover figure detail from 'Golden earring' by Gregg Kreutz reproduced with kind permission. ©Gregg Kreutz www.greggkreutz.com

Printed and bound in Great Britain by 4edge Ltd.
Papers used by Indigo Dreams are recyclable products made from wood grown in sustainable forests following the guidance of the Forest Stewardship Council.

for my Father

Also by Jenny Mitchell

Her Lost Language, IDP, 2019

CONTENTS

Foreword: A Brief History of Europe in Jamaica   9

The Master
Map of a Plantation	11
Master Plan	13
Naming the Slaves	14
There Will Be No Rebel Women	15
Prohibition Against Love	16
Burden of Ownership	18

The Maid
Lot 48	20
Minnie's Lament	22
When Mistress Speaks	23
Mastering Her Landscape	25
Wanting to Know Freedom	26
I Am the Song	27

The Mistress
First Draft	29
I've Heard of Them with Nails	31
It Came Out of Me as Stone	32
A Gentlewoman	33
Hunter	34
The Book Room	35

The Overseer
The Overseer's Tail	37
A Manservant Speaks/A Maid Transforms	40
Another Slave Lament	41
Plainly Master's Wife	42
Her Remains	43
The Craftsman	44

The Late Master

Master Can't Be Cured	46
Testimony of a Nurse	47
Bed of Languishing	48
The Late Master	49
Hummingbirds	50
Preparing the House for the New Master	52

The Nurse

The New Master in Confidence	54
In the Birthing Room	55
Sweet Joe Pye	56
Falling from a Leaf	57
Bending Down to Worship	58
Death of a Slave	60

The Fire

Death of the Final Master	62
We Dig the Master's Grave with Song	63
Domicide	64
Found Image of the Rebels	65
Putting Out the Fire Dance	66
John Crow's Feast	67

The 1838 Proclamation of Emancipation That Ended Slavery

69

Memorial

Another Vision of the Goddess	72
How I Write About Enslavement	74
Imagining a Forest Made of Freedom	75
Encountering a Slave Girl Held	76
Here Lies a Woman	77
Our Mother the Cartographer	78

Map of a Plantation

Foreword

A brief history of Europe in Jamaica

Xaymaca is the indigenous Arawak name for Jamaica, and means the land of wood and water. It is the third largest island in the Caribbean, after Cuba and Hispaniola, and was held under Spanish occupation from 1509 to 1655. The enslaved indigenous population was decimated by enforced labour and European diseases.

During Spanish domination and from 1655, when the island came under English (later British) colonial rule, African people were 'imported' and enslaved. Their labour ensured that Jamaica became a leading sugar exporter, based on a plantation economy.

The enslaved people did not officially gain their freedom until Abolition in 1838. Enslavement was replaced with a negotiated 'settlement' that established a system of apprenticeship. It tied the newly 'freed' men and women into another form of unfree labour for fixed terms. It also granted more than £20 million in compensation, (approximately £20 billion today), to be paid to the former enslavers.

At the same time, the formerly enslaved people were given no money, no land and no compensation. This, along with the 'importation' of Indian and Chinese indentured labourers by the British colonial rulers, ensured that the majority black population remained largely underemployed and impoverished.

Jamaica was a British colony until 1962. Its economy is heavily dependent on tourism from Europe and America.

Map of a Plantation

Unfurled, the ink is bright
four corners white as lace.
Not relic of the past
directions for the future.

Most prominent – a boundary
serpentine. God laid down to rest.
Look closer. He has vulnerabilities –
a gate dashed on the ground.

The trail leads not to fields
drawn golden as the sun.
Black bars criss-cross
to indicate a jail next to a graveyard.

Dots define the dead, leading to a dump
sketched to evoke a seething hill.
The chapel school is headed by a banner –
God protects the ones who kneel.

A treadmill like a thumbprint
challenges proportion
beside a colony of shacks.
The threat of heat in one

might lead to conflagration.
On towards a jagged crop
divided by pink streams. The blood
red roses in straight rows

point towards an ornamental garden.
Morning glories
frame a white house
guarded by an English oak.

This giant is the hanging tree
apt symbol of a master.
He dominates the map.
Roots creep along a path.

Master Plan

I'll kick all flowering plants to death.
Stamp petals into mud. Chop fruitless trees.
Destroy the flora I can't name.
Drink rivers, streams.

I'll shoot the brightest birds.
Their colours are too strange, the songs too loud, too lively.
They must not own the sky. Its sunlight and the heat
shimmers in the air as if it can't be caught.

I'll catch it with my mouth to name the places on the map.
Shout and with each word mark the edge of my estate.
Weaker men will do the work.
Progress shall be made.

Naming the Slaves

Half the fun of going to the quarters –
seeing a new batch in chains
eyes daring till I whip the ground
show them what a lick might do to skin.

Strongest men are named to mock
Pleasant
Cupid
Simply.

Women can't be treated lightly
though they might not look as strong.
When they scream, the thickest chain
seems to be a piece of thread.

Names must tell them what's expected –
Patience
Industry
and *Love*.

There Will be No Rebel Women

As master I will name them swamp / every shade of brown
sinister as mud / born for me to wade / taming with a whip
running at them hard / lash / a firebird

Force them into bed / all they have is mine / skin and blood and bone
won't abide their sound / shriek to rip through walls
fly into the air / aim for the high branches

Watch me snap / crow / pull them down / stamp underfoot
grind / my boot / blood spilt / rustle of red leaves / tamped
inside the mouth / rebel voices / lost

Prohibition Against Love

Advice to Masters and Overseers on Dealing with Their Slaves

1.
Free expression of the voice cannot be allowed.
Who hasn't seen the backbone of the Lord
in the way they stand, heads thrown back to push out song?
Could you slaughter cows that made you think of hope?

Imagine this – a day, quite normal like the rest.
You raise a hand to whip them into cringing shape.
They rent the air with *Glory Hallelujah! God is the Divine!*
Such elevated contents of the mouth might give you pause.

That's the way it starts. We must root it out.
Raise a whip to cooing. Rub salt in their lilting.
They must forfeit song at birth, sound reduced to pain.
Tamp it in the throat, hope it dissipates.

2.
It may prove impossible to stop a voice for long.
Birds have restless wings. Streams will do their flowing.
They can be controlled – birds kept in a cage
water plugged by stones, forced in new directions.

We must train their minds to think of words as threat.
A line of script looks like a path laid down in ink.
Education is good land. It must lead them to a jail
where the young are kept whilst parents work.

Learning has to be a chore, caned and not encouraged.
Money is well-spent on bibles. Let that be their only book.
It will teach them God is white, prayers another way to beg.
Keep the blacks down on their knees, never to rise up.

3.
What about their hearts – the right to swoon in love?
We must beat that nonsense out as a waste of time.
If they grow too tender with their young
trouble will be caused when selling off.

Fill their bodies with such pain, gentleness will irritate.
Wise men know it's true – those who suffer most
cannot bear the kindest touch. Beating with a whip
softens up the skin, tenderness like pawing at a wound.

Either way it's certain – slaves must not know love
long for sweet bouquets. They are meant to labour, breed.
Children have to answer to the name of *beast*.
Nothing more to add. Pass it on to generations.

Burden of Ownership

He measures cost in body parts. A head pays
for a month of food; two eyes, a week of drink.
Christmas adds a throat, carved out with care
the neck still holds a yoke if the chin is firm
weight evenly proportioned.

Four breasts pay for this season's clothes – a mad
extravagance he means to make the norm.
His furniture demands a score of navels.
One manly chest is paid for every horse.
He only wants the ones with heart.

Below the waist is worth the price of land – an acre
for two wombs. Twelve manhoods buy a gushing stream
to serve his house and fields. A sack of feet placed
yearly in a bank account maintains his balance
and the boast – he's always in the black.

Lot 48

There is no room to fall
though cliffs are promising
me waves.

A likely specimen, you'll all agree.

I'd sacrifice my knees to God
if He would form a path
through men.

Don't push. You'll have a chance to touch.

They're mute as bidding starts –
a cage of rank, pipe-smoking breath
held for the trader's voice.

We won't get far unless you offer more.

His words are loud
with number storytelling
smiling strong at four bids in a row.

Though black, her shade is comely.

He points towards my naked self
to make them look
too hard through skin.

She'll breed strong sons to work your fields.

The man who wins
pulls hard my hair
a crop he means to reap.

Don't hurt until your money changes hands.

Forced to look up
I see fast clouds
none covering my shame.

Lot 49. Who'll start the bidding?

Minnie's Lament

first day in the fields / forced into a row / women chop the cane
        hands turn into blood / legs / dead weight / each step
a punishment / not walking this but crawl / bundle on my head
        bones crack / haul a bundle to the cart / stop / breathe / eyes
close / overseer calls me / *beast* / whips a fire on my back / collar tight
        with sweat / *help* thrown in the dirt / towards the second day
shoes worn thin / pin my dress in front / no modesty in rags
        overseer calls me / *beast* / used to have a name / rat king
hurries past / sacks of squealing dirt / tails tied together tight / women
        run and scream / whip held in the air / overseer beats the king
conch shell calls a break at noon / water / chipped enamel cup / hard
        dough bread soaks up my sweat / easier to stand and eat
sitting there will be no strength / rat king comes again / bites
        the overseer's legs / hear the big man scream / smile
to move my lips / know my name again / forced into the fields
        forced to chop the cane / forced towards the third day

When Mistress Speaks

Lord God, I crave she words
bright gold in the mouth.
Oh, to have she riches!

Now I clean them house
there should be some pay,
a key set on my tongue

to tell the master *No*
he cannot come again.
My bed is mine.

How the mistress stay so rank
knowing that he take I pride
rob I inner strength?

Me? I'd like to turn a thief
steal *Ornate* as she names cloth.
Fill my pockets with *Flamboyant*

take out to the slave house as a gift
throw down on the fenky-fenky floorboards
make the softest rug

turn that buguyaga place into a palace
simply as I own the *A*
that begins she alphabet.

There will be *Acceptance*
under both my feet.
I will walk too proud for any maid.

Let she rooms stay nasty.
All I want is *Dainty*.
It will show me how to lie

upon she red chintz sofa
cock my cheeny finger
taking cups of tea.

Craven for the whites is weak
as she calls me when I run
from the hard lash of her hand.

Craven for we blacks is greed.
I will turn she words to food
nyam the pretty-pretty sounds.

Lord, if I can speak like she
will you close your eyes?
Take me to the promised land?

Mastering Her Landscape

After the last beating
he talks about his dreams, hunched
on the bed, hands in his lap
to hold the weapon down
even as the room spins red.

They always start the same.

Body I call mine
hangs by a thread.
Eyes move with the effort of my will
to search out light. It falls
as I once did, jagged near the door.

My house becomes a hill.

Two steps would be escape
but as he owns my legs
I'd have to float
above. His smell
sweats out of corners.

Funny how the trees grow taller.

He stands with all his might
as eyes I move
look far above his head
towards the distant trees
beyond the distant hills.

Wanting to Know Freedom

I went down to a stream
Watched it travel easy over rock

Glory was the sound it made
Calm the way it looked

Even as I leant towards the water
Urged it to go faster

Wanted more than anything
To push it with my hands

But the stream pushed back
As a mother might

Firm nudge and it was gone
Returned. Transformed.

I Am the Song

Despite a prohibition against love
laid down in myriad ways by the slave masters,
blacks only being born to work and breed,
a maid and a manservant stop one day
look each other in the eye. Speak soft words.
Hold hands when no one else can see her blush.
Arrange a day to meet far from the house.
Sit close together in the forest, kiss.
The grass beneath them does not mind the crush,
and fireflies come close to light their skin
as trees bend even closer, warmed by flames.
They do not rage. They smoulder. For a while
our couple lie together as if one
to tell us of their deepest thoughts, their dreams.

> He is the first I've known to touch me soft
> a stroke that does not ball into a fist or seek
> to hold hard when I push away – my need
> to breathe beyond the need to love.

> She turns her back to curve towards moonlight.
> Grim sky becomes smooth skin. I stroke again,
> trace every scar, whip-caused, becoming stars.
> They fall as I feel shame, cured to hear her sigh.

> His touch becomes a chant. I am the song
> returning to his arms. We're strong again.
> The master cannot hurt. A love like ours
> will lead to freedom – I am almost certain.

Our bodies work themselves into a sweat.
We find release and both call out *escape*.

First Draft

Dear Mother,

I'm sorry it has taken all this time to write but I'm still shocked at how the days go quickly in the heat. The wedding service went off well, although it was too close for such a massive gown. As you wisely said, I must adjust. The master's wife can't be too sensitive. ~~He stays out late and comes back drunk. I'm not to ask about his other women.~~

Is London changed at all? Tell father not to pine for me too much. I miss you both but there are compensations. The house is as we thought, a palace with more rooms than I can count. ~~Insects fly up to the chandeliers at night, sizzle as they burn, fall onto the floor or worse, the tablecloth. It makes me jump to crunch them underfoot.~~

I've had so many gifts the rooms are almost squalid. My husband, strange to write those words, is keen to buy a crib. He's even thought of names, convinced our first will be a son. ~~The marriage bed is soft with woodworm. Every night I pray he will not bother me again.~~ *Every morning brings a new adventure of some kind.*

My social life has never been so busy. We are the leading lights amongst the white elite. I wish I could describe how elegant their houses look, but none as grand as ours. It makes me very proud to be his wife. ~~He hit me yesterday for the first time and cried. It seemed like hours till he stopped. His head was heavy on my lap.~~

I think that anyone who saw our carriage would be envious. The stable has a dozen horses. Most of them are fierce but I possess a yearling. ~~He says I must not ride too far away. The slaves keep up attempts to run. He hunts them down to hang out on the lawn or place in stocks. I've heard the screams but have to learn to bear it.~~

My trousseau is more beautiful than anything I've ever owned. A seamstress visits once a month. She charges more than anyone in London but has the latest styles. ~~He chooses all my clothes, insists he'd be a laughingstock if I was left to do the job. A maid puts spiders in the wardrobe every night to eat the moths or they will eat the silk.~~

We rode out yesterday so I could see the whole estate, surrounded by the highest boundary wall. The slaves stopped working in the fields to bow. I waved until my husband said I had to stop. ~~He shouted and the women turned away as if they pitied me. I'll make them pay for those soft looks in time.~~

That's all for now. My fondest love.

I've Heard of Them with Nails

It is a well-known trick – men lie
upon a mattress made of spikes
such pressure on the skin
though blood they say is rare.

Reminds me of the marriage bed
longed for till he yanked my wrist
placed me underneath – pierced saint
stigmata high between my legs.

Pain forms in the dark, stains sheets.
On that first night, he named me
a stuck pig, half-slaughtered cow.
I prefer the princess and the pea.

My skin, though once as soft
is now a stretching wound.
He says a wife must bear
her husband's every need.

It Came Out of Me as Stone

The child. Dead weight. At first
rock quarried in my spine
until he slipped like moss
not green but slick.

Above his chin, a dent
as if a stone had cracked. Open
to a suckling mouth.
Milk came out as slurry.

A Gentlewoman

She throws a shadow on the morning
Glories in her flower bed

Bends to yank the fullest life
Out of land she names as dirt

Places every stalk inside a swinging basket
Pall-beared on her arm

Smiling at this murderation as the crows stare down
Knowing she's their kind in human form

As she stamps the blighted roses
Till their colours scream

Walks triumphant to the house
Puts the dead to stand in glass.

Hunter

That first year – the master's wife. Her voice flew
high enough to touch the ceiling. Wings beat hard.
Now a cry for help escapes the bedroom door.
I hurry to my work. Master will attack a maid who cares.

Every sound she makes is packed in tight.
I see his hands around her neck. He pins her to the wall.
She squawks like some great fowl
threatened by a hunter with his gun.

I sigh to clean the house and hear her scream.
Words are only said when master is not home.
High-pitched, she follows me from room to room
her voice become the hunter with his gun.

The Book Room

Come close. I have to whisper,
not meant to talk but dust.
The mistress will no longer speak.
I've learnt the words elective mute
by listening at cracks.

When doctor came from town,
her mouth gaped as he peered.
There was only teeth and tongue.
Nothing to explain, he said
how her mouth became a grave.

Master did not seem to mind.
Once, her words were sharp,
made him blush as if a child.
Now he struts and boasts
she cannot talk him quiet.

The day when she picked silence,
he slapped her hard in front of me,
pulled harder-still as if to steal her hair.
Let go bounced on the floor
where he knocked her down.

Words failed to stand again
no matter how he shook.
I thought her bones might break.
She climbed upstairs, all weary-like.
The book room has been closed for days.

I come to dust as an excuse
to steal his maps
set out a path
I mean to take
away from this plantation.

The Overseer's Tail

It happened the first time he beat a child –
a new job on a new plantation.
Happened all at once – the sorry curving of his spine
as if by bending down to whip a narrow, cringing back
the overseer bruised a muscle of his own
or something cricked.

Burdened with a stoop, he felt elated
when master praised his brutal work,
said he only had to beat the children from now on.
The overseer was so glad to do this job.
In just one night, his hands had lost some strength
fingers bent and tight.

It made him fear the adult slaves might turn against him
if they knew. He beat their children happily
not feeling his own pain.
Damaged them for days
until the master lost some profit in the fields.
After that, the broken little workers were easy to control.

The overseer grabbed two orphaned siblings –
a boy of eight, a girl of six, both stripped and made to kneel.
He smiled down from a wooden chair
the whip across his lap
feet planted like a king upon a throne
a pocket watch in his left hand.

He used the right to slap each child in turn,
teach them both the time.
Master wanted them to feel such fear
they wouldn't dare be late for work out in his fields.
With every blow, the boy looked shocked much more than scared
as if he hoped for something more.

The overseer hit again until the girl spoke out
in order to defend her brother. She earned the threat of worse,
looked down and ate her words.
When the children were dismissed in tears,
the overseer struggled to stand up
and walk back to his lair.

His stoop was now an aching crouch
hands so tight he dropped the whip. Against his will
he barked as hairs, coal-black and needle-thick
pushed out of his calloused palms.
Pain ripped through his arms.
A weight pressed both his shoulders even more.

His spine curved like a bowing bridge, pushed him on all-fours.
Screaming and in tears, he saw the worn-out
leather handle of the whip in front of him
snaking like a giant tongue regurgitated.
Mad with cracking bones, blood dampening his clothes
he thought the whip might beat the anguish out

edged towards it and collapsed,
chin hard on the floor. The handle nudged his lips
pushed against his teeth, broke the bottom row.
He screamed for help but moving forward
made the handle slide along his tongue.
He tried to cough it out, pulling at the whip.

It slithered down his throat to rent his heart
gouge through lesser organs, splitting guts to rip his arsehole
tear through cloth. He tasted bile mixed with the tang of shit.
The tip of his new tongue flopped from a red raw mouth.
He wanted death but clung to life, back arched in the air.
A tail thumped on the floor.

A Manservant Speaks/A Maid Transforms

My love and I escape along the path,
her left hand held so gently in my palm,
the right hand placed above her swelling gut.
Our child will know free land. It lies ahead.

The trail leads us towards the boundary wall.
When birds swoop down, we bat them all away
to fly through trees. Low branches snag her hair,
fight clothes to make us crouch, push forward.

We conjure up the wall with our deep breaths.
But dogs are coming close. They do not bark,
they curse as if the overseer's voice
is loud enough to make us stop, lose strength.

I feel his whip like fire on my back.
Her left hand falls. Men run to pull her down.

> I fold the land inside as I'm pulled down.
> Roll streams, a gushing flow placed in my mouth
> swallow till I'm free to breathe again
> the broken path divided into teeth.
>
> Men lift me up and trees become my hair.
> It's laden with each flower on this land
> hibiscus for the love I left behind.
> White orchids on my breasts become his hands.
>
> I'm taken to a cell and made to strip.
> No light but it is clear my skin has changed
> not dark and soft as fertile ground must be.
> No orchids but two chains become my breasts.
>
> When I look up, the roof turns into sky
> each cloud, my child, sent to the far horizon.

Another Slave Lament

I have known a key.
Such weight has touched my palm
doors opened with a turn.

This one says *Stop* – squat brass
jammed in the lock
on the other side.

A manacle around my neck
is nothing like a necklace
soft ornament to flatter skin.

I'm held by a short chain.
The overseer pulls. His laugh
sounds like a dog in this low light.

A woman starts to scream
until it hurts my throat.
I stop to feel the aching.

Plainly Master's Wife

Sitting at the looking glass, she blinks towards a blur.
It becomes her face. Wipes away the powder.

Ruddy cheeks annoy her as do fireflies
tapping at the windowpane. Slaves

in nearby quarters, free from overseers, scream.
Rouge stains on her dressing gown. Collar must be scrubbed.

Men bark on the lawn. Feral, they unleash a growl.
It becomes the overseer's voice, *Time to hang a runaway*.

Rose buds on the curtains have begun to fade.
Paint peels from the skirting.

Shadow in the looking glass. Comb falls on the floor.
Spider web of hair gathered by the wardrobe.

Hard to understand a maid who would dare to run.
She was given all a black deserves, even time to bear a child.

It will grow to be a maid. Tell her of this day
when her mother paid the price to a length of rope.

Does that scream belong to her? Slaves keen in their shacks.
Let the body rot. It will be fair warning.

Her Remains

She's become the hanging tree – a giant
oak the master meant to stop
all runaways.

Her dress helps shape high branches
bodice in mid-air –
a morning cloud

shifting to light blue – the rippling gown.
Arms flap empty wings –
circling of birds.

Buttons at the back – acorns to the waist
opened to expose five welts.
Master did not think

hanging was enough.
Hears her voice at night.
Calls it a faint breeze.

The Craftsman

A carpenter much more than slave
father grows the desk from his bare hands.
He'd like to build a ladder but avoids the boundary wall.
Says it bays for human blood – threat
to keep me safe. Mother tried to climb.
Sacrificed to rope.

I watch him plane a knot, carve legs from a trunk,
polish till his hand gleams like the top.
Slowly, he begins to talk, says my name so softly.
Mary, you were taken from her breast.
I was made to watch. Rope around her neck –
everlasting punishment.

Master says about the desk, *Yes. It's very good.*
Doesn't offer any pay. Father calls it, *Priceless*.

Master Can't Be Cured

He hasn't seen his naked body in a mirror for a while
but here's the mottled skin, the blue raised veins.

Hanging down between his legs, the sad remains –
what was called a man nestled in grey pubic hair.

His hands are gnarled, the knuckles misaligned.
Thin shoulders bear the weight, a balding head.

Weak arms might never hold another whip,
place rope around a neck. The ones he killed

tap on the windowpane, each hand a branch
that must be cut. They grow again. Tap every night.

Testimony of a Nurse

This room falls to its knees now master's weak
his ashen breath flaked on the furniture.
Bones try to conquer skin. The bed sags older.
No one says I might grow sick as him.

The door calls for escape through its thick oak.
Beyond is safety from a creeping touch.
I'd gladly run. Instead, his hand pulls mine
stone placed on top of all my scant protection.

A cry goes up to God and meets the ceiling.
His hand, no longer stone but a tight chain
is all the sickness clamped down on my fingers.
His cough becomes me too as I bend old.

Yet he demands a smile to keep him cheered.
I wear the mask pressed tight against my lips.

Bed of Languishing

Death is close enough to touch
him lying flat, breath choked,
hair a shock against the pillow
damp with sweat.
Wasted arms reach up to take my hand
black against his wan.

I cannot go too close
for fear it is contagious.
His head rolls back, neck baby weak.
He whispers *Help*,
the struggle in his mouth
like chaos saying every prayer.

Come darkness, he is lying straight
to fit a coffin, sheets a wrinkled lining.
I wash his body, fragile as a child,
watch him like a mother praying for her son.
The Lord will strengthen him
upon a bed of languishing.

Come morning, he attempts to shout
my name – his final word.
The corpse is taken out.
I change the sheets, lie down.
No one comes to hold my hand.
I'm left upon a bed of languishing.

The Late Master

Some say he was a ravening bird
who feasted on the bodies of his slaves.
The truth is more prosaic – a stooped
and shuffling man, prematurely grey.

His clothes just never seemed to fit.
He suffered with his feet, both bunions and corns.
Sleep disturbed towards the end
he rose before the cock began to crow.

The nurse who cared for him laughed
there were bottles everywhere.
He wet himself at night
mattress rank with piss.

Some say he's gone to hell – well, yes
if hell is six feet underground
in a small teak box. He chose that wood
because it withstands termites.

Hummingbirds

Strike me if I lie, mistress has become a garden.
Days since master's death, the whip he held
slips from her twiggish hand as she falls down.

I help her into bed, pick up the whip, first time
not fearing licks for breathing the same air.
Her skin, once pale, is now a weeping rash.

She takes my hand as if she's never shouted *wretch*.
Orders me to bathe her in the bed, tender with a back
once stiff as oak, flopsy on the sponge.

She mumbles to my breasts how pain is not deserved.
I bathe her, yes, but long to whip that soul to death.
Instead, I hold a pillow to her face, grit my teeth

step back to hear a choking sound, pillow on the floor.
All at once, her mouth becomes a rose.
Eyes, once grey and hard, are hummingbirds.

I fall down on my knees, crawl from the room.
Lord God is thrown downstairs till I shake quiet,
no movement in the house, like night takes off its shoes.

I creep towards the bed as knotweed pushes through her palms.
Praying hard, I tell myself to stamp the mistress-garden
deep into the soil, or tend as if she grows for me.

I fetch pure water from the stream to pour along her legs –
a mass of roseleaf bramble, prickly to the touch.
Her trunk is made of oak, breasts a hill of fallen leaves.

Nettles grow out of her gut, a flowerbed beneath.
The sun comes in the room but only gentle heat
to warm my skin and help this garden grow.

I love the Eden she's become so close to laying in the ground.
Her eyes, those wondrous birds, stare back at me
most mornings. I call their song my daily glory.

Preparing the House for the New Master

We empty the latrine of bones – pure alabaster.
Skin brought up in shreds is brown, slopped
on the ground with other waste – a black child's song,
a neck once snapped by rope, ribcage pulled apart.

Out flies a bird, its cry, a woman's scream.
There are other sounds wretched in the rags
the master used to wipe his arse. Lost stories
of escape bubble to the surface.

The New Master in Confidence

You must have heard black women are for work,
mixed-breeds offer sex, white women kept for marriage.
It is true. Fields are full of dark ones with their sweat. Stained
dresses speak of filth between their legs.
A man must pull out riches from this swamp
throw away what can't be used.

Brats are put to work at six years old. Why not five?
Mothering is damaging my crop, limiting the fields.
If I sell weak children off, women will attack. Overseers
have to use more threat. Mixed-breeds are the ones to trust.
Even in the house they seem less ape, more human.
Here there is a nurse, black enough to scrape.

Never seen a smile but a pretty face.
I will break her will on a strong brass frame.
Then I'll go to town, find a sepia mistress.
She must have soft hair, bright eyes. Light-skinned
children can be used to serve inside my house.
They shall call me father when we are alone.

If I choose a wife, I shall send to England.
Cold makes them genteel enough to decorate my house.
She must never know the nurse
breeds for me strong sons and daughters
bound to be too dark to keep.
They will make a profit when they're sold.

In the Birthing Room

My baby starts to push – flesh stabbed
inside. I hold a scream as that's the law –
not written down – the common sort.
Slaves are sold if we aren't strong.

I dare not cry above the master's stable.
His horses might grow wild, buck walls.
He calls them Pride and Joy. I am *Girl* and *You*,
made to bow as he walks past.

Pain tears blood between my legs. I try to stand
reach down to touch the aching crown but fail.
An overseer's wife has tied my hands – an order
from the master. He lost a profit long ago.

A girl like me grabbed for her new born son
dashed him on the floor, cracked dead
before he could be branded, chained.
I'd never hurt my young though forced to bear.

It might resemble master. He'll be kind.
A girl could act as maid, a boy as groom.
These jobs are dreams of glory. I'm worn thin.
At seventeen, my back aches all the time.

Dreams are lost as I buck hard.
A final stab. My child
flops on the bed as I fight rope.
She's taken up, sold to another parish.

Sweet Joe Pye

Slave Mary has possessed the land
master cannot use to grow his white gold cane
beside the stocks and the latrine.

Here she breeds a garden, plants named for her children.
Angelica was the first driven into Mary's womb.
Master broke her on a large brass frame.

Swelling belly was a curse. Pain between her legs
in the birthing room. Baby fell on rotting planks.
Bud-like lips sought heavy breasts

till a trader came, plucked the young away.
Mary cursed. The master dragged her to the stocks.
In chains, she watched plants grow in waste

saw a way to have her stolen child.
Now Angelica's profligate. Mary does not know the word
cannot write the plant is proud as Sunday hats.

Boasts about her other offspring – Sweet Joe Pye
the favoured one despite his slouch.
Butterflies adore the boy, adorn the small pink buds.

Primrose is the next one down but she likes to be alone.
Over there is Clary Sage, purple too, a calming force.
Jasmine grows so delicate. Mary knows to tend with care.

Lily Bay, the sunshine girl. As the youngest, she is spoilt.
An entire orange path leads to a tin shack.
Mary leans out of the window late at night.

Sings a self-made lullaby, *Grow, my children, grow.*
Smiles to watch them sway as they say goodnight.
The name they use does not begin with slave.

Falling from a Leaf

I see the likes of you, look at the likes of me
as only this – a slave in rags, skin like mud
shack held up by dirt and hope.

That is not the end. That is not the start.
I used to be a bible woman, rang a bell for God
knew his words by heart, though I cannot read

verse and psalm repeated in the church
till it seemed a frog, croaking I must kneel
offer thanks despite my children sold.

As the last was taken from my breast, I cursed God
quietly or the master will attack
as if a crime to hate the life he steals.

I cursed him good as well, raving near my shack
hoping in my heart God would strike me dead
till I saw the light fall from a leaf

followed it towards the garden I have grown
must grow again by kneeling down
to worship what is found in mud.

Bending Down to Worship

Church Mary said her God was in the ground
not Satan but all the things that grew,
and flowers were the gems upon His crown.
She made a garden all around her house –
a broken shack she called a palace
where she reigned.

You couldn't step beyond her door
unless you brought her a bouquet
or something green and pulsing full of life.
She filled each bowl and glass she found
with blooms she called her jewels
though they were better as they gave a lovely scent.

She tended to her tiny Eden
till the flowers reached above her head –
the colours bold against dark skin, so filled with shining light.
Her headwraps were bright floral wreaths
and every dress was made of faded flowers
the age-old shoes like clumps of mud.

On days when she was forced to work out in the fields
she feared the sun might scorch her garden.
She ran out of the cane the moment that the whistle blew
and went to fetch pure water from the stream.
Her flowers had to live
as they were all the freedom that she knew.

On nights when she was grieving
she went outside to kneel amongst the plants
bend her head and talk to God.
He answered back by showing her another rock or stone
she had to move, revealing yet more ground
on which to grow more buds.

One Sunday as the white priest tried to make her go to church
she offered him her shining patch of land
with one sweep of her arm.
She said, *I never saw your Jesus,*
but when I die, I'll end up in the ground
to feed the things I love to grow
and that is all the heaven I will need.

He damned her as a Godless slave.
But when he left, she heard the voice of God again.
He spoke to her of flowers
as she bent to ornament His crown.

Death of a Slave

Church Mary tells weak legs to take her to the garden.
Her back with little strength, cricks, settles near the plants.
Flowers in her head-wrap droop – Queen Anne's lace –
white buds on the wedding gown she never owned, her life
strapped to the master's bed.

Sunshine mimosa, over there – a dark pink patch
grows tall before her eyes, sways softly in the breeze.
She strokes the leaves so tenderly. They fold
too sensitive for any touch as she has been –
the master's hands were hoary, rough.

A flight of butterflies, red flames above the lavender
fragrant and so wild. She prays for it to cover all the land –
a final gift for her six children sold.
Eyes dim, she sees this offspring up ahead.
It is not a dream. She hurries on towards them.

Death of the Final Master

The undertaker says the smell is too diseased
for an aged man of natural causes.
No punctures to his frame and yet
an odour like a charnel house. Crow-black
suit, a brittle crust. It snaps
as they undress the corpse
bone-thin in life, risen like a loaf.

Sharp features spread across his face,
veins bulging to the surface.
Hair, once sparse, grows thick
as rope across the pillow.
Slaves move close to keen.
Cheer instead to see the devil
come to claim his own.

We Dig the Master's Grave with Song

A soaring hymn changed to a hum. The overseer cannot hear
there's glory in each clod, a chorus formed from dirt.
It flies as we repeat our work, elation falling in the mud.

We dig again to make a twelve-foot hole – six for the man
who died in pain, loud cries sent out across the land fenced in.
Six more for the devil who held sway, a whip in his right hand.

Glory Hallelujah to the ground! We heft him in at last,
coffin made of song covered with free verse. As notes ascend
the mound we walk upon becomes an ever-lasting chant.

Domicide

The master's house was born and lived a hundred years
before the slaves break in to roam throughout the rooms.

They only want to sit in comfy chairs, kick away their shoes
know the softness of his rugs. Softness is so rare

it makes them dwell on their hard work, the children sold.
Men stand to tear the portraits off the wall, break trinkets

on the mantle, throw books from the shelves, bend spines
dash across the floor, stamp the words to dust.

A desk with ornate legs is sacked, documents thrown in the air.
The soup tureen is used for human waste, cutlery divided up.

Women run into the master's room, rip linen off the bed
as if it is his flesh, rags thrown on the newly-ruined lawn.

An oak tree's axed as men attack the wardrobe till it shakes.
They wear the master's clothes, fight for his shoes

throw aside the handkerchiefs as they are monogrammed.
That looks branded, someone says, just like the skin.

There isn't any money in the house which seems just typical.
But there are handles made of brass and copper piping.

After it is stripped, everything is set alight. The people
do not stay for long to watch the structure burn.

Found Image of the Rebels

They're captured in a field
arranged in careful rows
height descending to the front.

Women with bare feet, skirts long
tops clearly darned
gaps exposing skin

hair hidden under wraps
plaits hanging loose or
pointing up like horns.

Men in weary shirts
no buttons till the waist,
frayed cuffs as if attacked by dogs.

Their skin has given all its sheen
to the sun-dappled crop –
forest of tall cane.

High up in the corner at the right
where the sun might sit –
a house inhabited by flames.

They cause the image to ignite.
It burns close to the edge
curling as the roof caves in.

But people in their rows
refuse to look
as walls begin to crack.

Putting Out the Fire Dance

1 August 1838 – Emancipation Day

I can't begin to talk about the men not knowing how to start
field hands in ragged clothes, they lumber
shadows through the church.
We women clap as boys weighed down with drums –
deep water underneath their hands
begin the noise. I can't describe. Heart beat
has never been so strong. It jumps
out of the skin to land at feet. Men shuffle, stop.
Begin to talk, high pitched as women are
when food is scarce or children pass.
Till overwhelmed by sound, the men stand quiet
except for long, deep breaths. It leads into a dance
beyond control. They slip off their torn shirts.
Drums are muscled backs. The church, makeshift and rough
poverty hewn in a Cross, grows wild
pews replaced by trees, sweat
falling like hibiscus leaves as men
move down the aisle – a stony path.
I'd like to say they undulate, not bones
inside of flesh but water. Look! Legs dart and sway
till all the hate they held so long
cascades towards we women
who have suffered at their hands.
Our pain transforms as we dance wild.
Men kneel and pray to us
pick up torn shirts – those ragged birds
fly high above the branches.

John Crow's Feast

> *Sirs, we must begin to carve with care.*

Food melts across a piled oak table – hanging tree, planed
polished. Glazed roast hog – a centrepiece to temp the guests –
Masters, Abolitionists, Members of the British Crown.
All begin to speak till one voice dominates.

> *Sirs, freedom is most delicate*
> *if we want to keep the slaves*
> *underneath in tumbling shacks*
> *owning nothing more than dirt.*

Ceiling fans whir their approval, fail to drown a distant hum –
fires set by black rebellion means there are no slaves to serve. Guests
must pour their wine, reach for food burnt-bland with a grudge
by idle wives forced to cook for the first time.

Now a master shouts,

> *Damn the blasted slaves,*
> *those beasts of burden.*

A leading Abolitionist stands up.

> *Sirs, may I interject?*
> *We're set upon a path*
> *where other names will be assigned –*
> *work-shy, disadvantaged, coon.*
> *For now, please call them free.*

Masters start to agitate until the British Crown holds forth.

> *Sirs, you will have compensation –*
> *twenty million pounds.*
> *Won't that be a laugh?*
> *First, grow rich out of black blood.*
> *Richer now they've won.*

Here, the guests grow tipsy to decide the settlement –
blacks will have no land, no rights.
Forced to stay on the plantations.
Forced to pay rent for the shacks they once had for free.

When the paper's signed, a leading Abolitionist speaks up.

> *Sirs, we must become the heroes of this tale.*
> *Blacks can't know it's them*
> *or they'll fight for more.*

As it is agreed, masters slice blancmange in equal thirds.

The 1838 Proclamation of Emancipation That Ended Slavery

A PROCLAMATION

By His Excellency Sir Lionel Smith, Knight Commander of the Most Honourable Military Order of the Bath, Knight Grand Cross of the Royal Hanoverian Order, a Lieutenant-General in Her Majesty's Land Forces, and Colonel of the Fortieth Regiment of Foot, Captain-General, Governor in Chief, and Commander of the Forces in and over Her Majesty's Island Jamaica, and other the Territories thereon depending in America, Chancellor, and Vice Admiral of the same.

Praedial Apprentices,

In a few days more you will all become Free Labourers — the Legislature of the Island having relinquished the remaining two years of your apprenticeship.

The 1st of August next is the happy day when you will become free — under the same laws as other free men, whether white, black, or coloured. I, as your Governor, give you joy of this great blessing.

Remember that in freedom you will have to depend on your own exertions for your livelihood, and to maintain and bring up your families. You will work for such wages as you can agree upon with your employers. It is their interest to treat you fairly. It is your interest to be civil, respectful, and industrious.

Where you can agree and continue happy with your own masters, I strongly recommend you to remain on those properties on which you have been born, and where your parents are buried. But you must not mistake in supposing that your present houses, gardens, or provision grounds, are your own property. They belong to the proprietors of the estates, and you will have to pay rent for them in money or labour, according as you and your employers may agree together.

Idle people who will not take employment, but go wandering about the country, will be taken up as vagrants, and punished in the same manner, as they are in England.

The ministers of religion have been kind friends to you — listen to them — they will keep you out of troubles and difficulties.

Recollect what is expected of you by the people of England, who have paid such a large price for your liberty.

They not only expect that you will behave yourselves as The Queen's good subjects, by obeying the laws, as I am happy to say you always have done as apprentices; but that the prosperity of the Island will be increased by your willing labour, greater beyond what it ever was in slavery. Be honest towards all men — be kind to your wives and children — spare your wives from heavy field work, as much as you can — make them attend to their duties at home, in bringing up your children, and in taking care of your stock — above all, make your children attend Divine Service and School.

If you follow this advice, you will, under God's blessing, be happy and prosperous.

Given under my hands and seal at arms, at Saint Jago de la Vega, this Ninth day of July, in the Second Year of Her Majesty's Reign. Annoque Dommi, One Thousand Eight Hundred and Thirty-Eight. ~ **Lionel Smith, By His Excellency's Command, C H Darling, Sec.**

Another Vision of the Goddess

The midwife paid to lay out the dead
swore the last field hand to be enslaved
was not just lined with age –
there were words – distinct as moles –
a whole book of female parchment
opened up beneath her neck.

The face was plain brown paper scrunched too small.
The corpse was underfed
but the words were fat and curling bold.
My father and our country
etched on her right shoulder,
My children sold across the left.

A cave spelt out on a sagging breast,
A winding path on the other.
Then placed beneath them both:
A hill went down to a bush.

I loved a man who loved me too
was scrawled across her gut.
Him killed in cane. I hid was caught –
these words were placed on both her legs
along with the names of all her masters
the fields she had to work.

Her knees were swollen
as if water dripped on paper – dried.
The letters spelt out, *Punishment.*
A rape.

I ran was written on one shin,
the other was left blank.
It did no good was printed across both feet.

There was nothing written on her back –
the spine immaculate
but dipping down towards her waist
the boldest script of all:
My mother prays with me at night.

The midwife gave her word,
faltered to explain
how all this writing disappeared.

How I Write About Enslavement

I dig bones from a grave carried on my back
lay them on the page – blood full-stops.
Chains are brought up next, a tangled weight.

Whips the overseers soaked in salt
start a fire on my skin. Deep wounds
turn into welts, flower into sentences.

My body folds, neck wrenched to feel the rope
pulling at my neck. Knees quake. Each organ
fills with names, the children sold

their cries tamped in my throat, locked away
for safety's sake until they scream
break free, demand a page.

Imagining a Forest Made of Freedom

They're bubbling, black roots reforming
pushing at the soil. Bones misshapen
with slave labour, straighten and grow strong
ripping through the ground.
Fractures caused by beatings fuse, shape young trees
swelling to enormous trunks, fed with blood unjustly spilt.
Welts, deep-planted by a whip, design a hardy bark.
Starvation in reverse makes fertile leaves
wave, carefree at last.

Encountering a Slave Girl Held

In a museum cabinet, glass-topped
abandoned coffin. Lying straight.
Thin-faced, bark-hued.
Plaits against her scalp except a reckless horn.

Eyes blink obsidian.
Quick movement of the mouth.
She's missing teeth or two in front. A hand cracks glass.
Slowly, she steps down, dress caught in the shards.

I back away as fingers work the jag, head lowered
left cheek bruised down to the chin she lifts with pride
exhibiting a rope burn –
choker set with gleaming coals.

Her voice cracks low – *This time, I will not leave my breath*
when I decide to run. Feet hardly dared
to touch the ground like waves
pulled out from under me.

This time, the trees will fold
bend bark knees.
No branch to snag my dress or point towards my back
surely as an arrow. I will aim

to reach the wall before it's dark.
Climb each brick, big as a baby's coffin.
No dog will bite my heel.
No rope turned to a choker.

Here Lies a Woman

My first time in Jamaica, I went searching
for her grave on an old plantation site –
house a white museum. Portraits of plump masters
next to cabinets with chains. A dainty whip
beneath a sign, *The handle of carved ivory
was made to fit a woman's hand.*

Near to the Union Jack, a flowing gown
placed on a mannequin, keys heavy at the waist
beside a box of rags, carefully arranged –
*Taken from the body of Church Mary
(family name unknown). One of several slaves
on this estate who self-destroyed.*

I walk the ghosts of fields next to a carpark
to a restaurant that used to be a jail.
Slaves worked a treadmill here until they died.
The windows with wide bars allow a balmy breeze
relief for lobster-coloured tourists
knuckle-deep in carbs.

They nod to reggae floating from the speakers.
It wafts along a dusty road the enslaved ran.
I stroll, the present day held back by weeping
willow trees, an avenue of dogwood. Leaves
trail towards a sudden sea, rocks like muscled backs.
On the mossy bank, a well-kept grave.

Etched across the headstone is the name *Church Mary*
above a fulsome epithet – *Here Lies a Woman
Constant as The Land. She planted flowers
for her children sold, the ones lost out at sea.
On nearing death, she took her life.*
I watch as children wave, go out, return.

Our Mother the Cartographer

lies down for the last time,
called a well-earned rest.
Body like a mountain range
spread across a hard-washed sheet
laid bare as the sun beams from her shape –
new delirium but not the worst.

She can see the father of her children –
man she knew as master –
pockmarked with his death,
float above the bed
arm raised to the ceiling –
called a dimming sky –
falling to etch scars upon her skin.

Here she draws us close – daughters
in the future
conjured by a fever.
Points towards the dip
between her breasts
calls it *A lost place of peace.*
Cups the sagging mounds.

These were never mine.
Forced to breed too many children.

Here, we have to kneel
anticipating mourning –
night has just begun.
Watch her belly rise.
Fall into a crater.

She heaves on her side –
flesh unsettled range.
Welts across her back are deep-kicked paths.

Yes, I tried to run.
Land beyond the gate belonged to him.

Now we start to keen
shrill as birds thrown in the air.
But she calls for quiet.
Voices settle on the floor.
As she lies back down
softly we can hear –
Trace a path until the end.

Acknowledgements and References

Poems in this collection have previously been published by or in association with Aryamati Poetry Competition, Bad Betty Press, Bread and Roses Poetry Award, Deep Time Poetry Anthology (Volume One), Dust Poetry Magazine, Ice Floe Press, Mineral Lit, Segora Poetry Competition, Versodove and Ware Poetry Competition.

'Naming the Slaves': the names in this poem are taken from archival records of enslaved people in Jamaica.

'Bed of Languishing': quotation from Psalm 41:3: *'The Lord will strengthen him upon a bed of languishing: thou wilt make all his bed in his sickness.'*

The 1838 Proclamation can be found at:
www.commerciallawinternational.com

All references to 'slaves' and 'masters' in this collection reflect the language used during the long period of enslavement. They suggest imposed/assumed titles which is why, outside of the poetry, the author prefers the terms enslaved, enslaver and enslavement.

Many thanks to Dawn Bauling, Julian Bishop, Ronnie Goodyer, Eve Gordon, Katharine Hoare, Gaynor Macdonald, Gill Scott, Ann Taylor and Wes White.

Thanks always to Nancy Christina Downie, Mark Anthony Mitchell, Margaret Rose Mitchell and Milton Williams.

Indigo Dreams Publishing Ltd
24, Forest Houses
Cookworthy Moor
Halwill
Beaworthy
Devon
EX21 5UU
www.indigodreams.co.uk